SPINE

a book of poems by

KAREN HANSON

an Ithaca House book

Ithaca

Some of these poems originally appeared in *Tri-quarterly*, *Epoch*, *Dialogue*, and *The Trojan Horse*. Acknowledgement is due to the editors of those magazines for permission to reprint.

Cover photography by Jill Morgan

ISBN 0-87886-009-6

ITHACA HOUSE
314 FOREST HOME DRIVE
ITHACA NEW YORK 14850

To Florence

CONTENTS

GROCERY

He goes to the grocery
and watches the fruit
Sitting in piles, in circles,
In curves and pineapple spines.

"Consider my cat Geoffrey," said Mr. Smart,
and this is also a Christmas carol.
Consider the mouse, he said.
Consider young lions and porpoises.
Think of them wrestling, diving and rising,
Or in the sun, think of them
on a television screen or even a photograph,
Stopped.
Consider curls, curves, and backbones.

There is the history of seashells and telephones.
The seashells take a long time, those
Larger than two fists, to arrive
In your room, and talk on
Even longer, windy, and telephones
Miraculous webs, we balance
and walk on our voices too, sparrows
Sway on the wires. Or lying down
in the car at night you can see
How continuously the lines
Move, (consider the car standing still)
And the low cut moon hangs
in them, on the table the receiver
is more than one voice at once,
a curved smooth bridge
and sparrows sway on the wire,
a seashell also is a receiver
of many voices, revolving
(and on this I would base my paper)
Yet there is no satisfaction that does not involve

More than one person.
In fond disorder.
Opening of doors.
And far out the oars lick the salt water
It runs off the oars shining
As on the beach the round crabapples sway
To the push
Of the white fingers
Of the waves

Whoever is growing bristles,
Whoever is growing strawberries,
Whoever is growing wool,
Whoever is growing milkweed
That now float
out of their arched boats with arched seeds
Below the miraculous web
of wires

Whoever is growing bristles
Whoever is growing coats
or fur, or the cool owls,
Whoever is growing doves,
or sweet lonely yells,
Whoever is growing roses

Bracelets and words
(for we have laughed together,
and on this I would base my paper)
Whoever is growing crabapples,
or even just making up new games
Whoever is growing eyes, or ears,
Watching, waiting
(and on this I would base my paper)

Or even just making up new games,
Please continue.
This is a celebration.
Miraculous webs.
Ferris wheel speed to electronic music.
How the seashell is a receiver too, revolving
Out of their arched boats with arched seeds
and there is something I would share,
and this is also a Christmas carol,
considering lions and porpoises.

He goes to the grocery
and watches the fruit.

WE LIVE IN MIRRORS

1

We live in mirrors but don't look in them.
Or else they are kaleidescopes of
Denial, maybe boredom, terror
I don't know
This is imagination at its worst
A meager sift of snow
While telephone rings really
Urgent bells occupy the livingroom.

The time came for us a moving out ceremony.

2

The mood is there
A kind of fierce animal
Tight fur, implacable
Snide eyes, knowing
Its own power.

Clocks waited around us, our hands
On the arm of phones, knob
Of doors.

3

To see yourself is to make faces,
To be able to open to others' making faces,
the games you hate or fear grow real.

Let us be.

4

Then it was summer
And the heat makes us sweat.
We move our time outdoors.
In offices they plot vacations.

Kyrie eleison
Hello willows
Go easy on those I love

5

For him the car waited
Impatiently in the driveway.

He kissed me but he was leaving so
                                        I leaped
Away and danced across the grass in the dark
And he came
After me, we ran
Together my laughter jumped
Out of my belly my laughter ringing
All round us

THE STANDING STILL JOURNEY

As I listen . . .
The loudness of the minutes ticking
in the clock of cut and tire and reflection
tunnels slowly
into silence.

Words' hands hold hard
to stays
of blank pages

From a distance
I hear voices going on
beyond the doors
the moments close.

I drag in the soft direction
Drain the weathers of their faces
Walk a sleep
                        to circumstance

                        Quiet
is over my head
and underneath my feet
and heavy
                    heavy
in the palms of my hands.

.
.
.

The shadow is in the wall,
ageless as a statue.

It will not leave
when the light leaves.

It holds a secret,
speaks in questions,
beckons . . .

The other side
of the hour
is the velvet
of the glass.

The other side of the hour
is velvet and the sharp
sand spilling sounds softer

than mouth   on   stone

.
.
.

Night's a funnel:
Fears rise like flowers
to luxuriate in the dark

and are drawn in.

If there's harvest, wine
of this calm, growing,
then the child blind in me
may drink of it only
by a cup made of her hands
covering my face.

POEM

As you walk on trees,
I travelled underground;
And were we upside down?
It's the same.

I took a rabbit's way, a spider's.
A mole-hill was a mountain,
but now I stand up, ass, adorned,
Complete with damns and sorries.

You and I are strangers, friend.
Your terror's true –
I bend for that.
Do you bend always
                    Away?

I'm back from the wars
(sister   sister)
With soft news: Nobody wins.
Nobody loses.
Nobody's there – nobody but
Moon, with his kindergarten
Grimace. And I'm here.
I'm not there.

HUNT

I

I saw a face in a stone,
I saw a wound in a dry man's eye.

He had nothing to say.
The ambulance was obvious, you

could hear it in the wind,
continuing, going

Away.
We were miles away from anywhere

Where blood might be shared,
though we all belonged to it.

It isn't as if I cannot see,
I said.

II

The color
of sadness. A covey
of wounds, behind the bush,

Blush not out.
Never be caught

Cut, mended,
kissed, or killed.

Wait
in silence –

To move at all
is to be discovered.

Huddle deep
in profuse cover –

the thickness of their nature
and their natural surroundings.

A family of them,
paralyzed by an instinct,
blind, watchful,
waiting, seeing
nothing –

But the denseness
of the thickets
they hide
within.

Wait
for the hunter,
anticipate his gun,

a grossness
of pain

Exposure

III

In a dream:

I go

behind my father
who goes to hunt in the fields
with his dog.

The brush is dense and we walk
slowly. The air is dry.
It is hard for the dog to scent
the birds in the wind.

I sense the warm of summer
receding in the changing shadows.
The season is Fall.
Chicory are closing in the sun.

The flower
of a burr
whispers to me.
I feel
what I watch
stir on its lips.

I bend to hear
what I need to be told.
The time is difficult.
The weather is disguising.
The clouds open and close
the sky. Sharp seeds
catch on our clothing.

We go
and we cannot tell
where they are, what we want,
whether we want or no.
I cannot tell if this is sport
or real. Or if he sees,
or I do, any better,
or if we care to see.

The birds hide, they are not easily uncovered.
They make no sound until they fly.
Then, they have no voices but their wings.

A dog is a near-blind beast,
and our eyes follow him,
and he follows
the smell of the wind.

We go
by his vestigial instinct,
knowing no name for hunger . . .
                                        The birds wait
                                        in the verges
                                        of fear

IV

The wind
whipped us
and wrapped us
at turns

The gun
struck us
and spoke us
Both –

      Each time
It broke itself
The spider spun bed
for feathers of birds
                    Held

When the gun
held its peace

and spilt
into the silence
Despair
                Cover caving
                        in,
                    falling

When the bullet broke
Through the thickening
                    air

Shriek of bird
and word
of gun:
                GROW

MORNING

We crowd into our candles,
like race car artists
Eager for speed, totality
Waiting
for the start

The line glows
Like the smell of you
When I turn to my special brakes
and can't find them

All our friends and we are in a circle
Arms around each other indiscriminately,
Laughing

I stand here
in the breakfast calm smoke
breathing your absence
Acknowledge three oranges
on the table

And all my little boats
Adrift.

PROSEPOEM

This preoccupation with dawn in painful to the mind
that cannot cling to change but will always be
bowing to the gracious sadness.
The flavor of the merrygoround is our disconnection.
That we need each other is true but not obvious nor the
obvious end.

Then I go walking, again, through this landscape of words which
is only a percentage landscape of my life which is a reaching out,
a drawing in, reaching out, drawing in

Am convinced there is no possible direct route to the obvious.
Perhaps it is possible to make immediate commitments as the fear
of loss grows. Still better to create the very situation you
stiffen from and then punch it as energetically as possible,
grasp, laugh, cry and tire to consider it a thing of the past.

These sentences are of the family that is raised innocently sly
for an always future affirmation, white eggs hid under the couch
cushion constantly replenished puzzlements, feeling filtered in
ever old new accumulatory ways so as not to be too sure and then
the slow blossoming of some pain and the arm stretched passionately
toward breakfast.

I want the time machine. Take me back to that one perfect
chance to get my hands on the condensed obstructions in one
ready pillow and this time I won't say uncle I promise no matter
how much you twist my arm.

Family of sentences that rise like bread but where? but
sincerely I told you I would make sacrifices in your name for
what good would I be if not my self but how? but truly I
circumscribed those resigned hollows with eggshells to break,
cut with, immediacy for replanting and your fearful presences
for the dominating goals because where would I go if not back

to people but to static insane ease and terror and an ungratefully runny tongue of which nothing could be made but why? Now I want to begin where language ends but where? Back to the briar patch with you.

Promises that aren't kept. Bravery that means coming back, going away. Do you search for the definite article? The place both stage and natural? The infinitely falling and rising in love and loss like waves that are one and the same and specially? Do you look upward to be beyond our half-lights so that you can enter them and be, being able to enjoy the tiniest darkroom, or the broadest demands that you should no longer be inadequate of meeting them or superseding them or lifting us all out of them and so no longer have to be apart or unapart of any of us, the tiniest darkroom, the heaviest bags? Is this why you hurt us with your leaving? In order to perfectly return? And who do you think you are? I love you. But how?

The act is what matters. Every glance at the coffee cup. Every joke in the pantry and on the road. Every enticement and every self-conscious minute-hour of silence at the questioning beginnings and the questioning endings, the question in-between times, the outsets of grief and relief, the outside times when we aren't inside what we're doing, neither together nor alone, but too conscious of the words. Feel me.

Don't tell me that wasn't a rifle shot. If one part is green, another is gray, and vice versa. I'm willing to laugh. The uses of trying, various, incredible, complex, come to me, come from me, we enter the sanctuary and are well pleased with the symphonies of a cafeteria, of rainy streets and the clinking of gutters, of money spenders with their flat brims, of the sinuous dancing of cool expert machines that have left us out what is there to cry over but we enter on wave-edges and decide it would well please us to expand our longing into a session of tears a half-hour conference with the plaster saints of what we have wanted and abandoned and persisted and mingled in our cookwork minds the once simple aliveness though the trip which

you are taking demands so much that goes against the grain
Whose grain? What grain? And it is as if we cut a path through
the packed trees like so much stacked oranges in a grocery bin
we are afraid there will be nothing left and someone appears
like the smile of the Cheshire cat to say that that's the point
and everything will begin there now is our disgust with where
we are and where the world is enough to take us there? Hope
actual and immediate hop on the back of the truck. We are
hitching out. I love you. Let us play.

3/65

Nowhere to end.
Nothing left to burn.

But the dark chords
Do not end
Where the keyboard
Stops.

I would wear another face.
This frozen flower of anger,
This winter of care

Cuts deep, cuts dear, kills . . .

Bitter,
Leaves bare
Nothing to begin

But the endless burial
    of broken stairways
        once descended

Down.

A SIGN

Often
there is an underfire.
The insistence of the dog
Who is after a fly. The hunt
Itself, one notices that, its tensed nostrils.

Don't starve your dog.
It will eat people up.

REPERTOIRE

Where is the repertoire?
A visit to the dentist.
How should he strike fear
in our hearts by asking questions
We can't answer because our jaws are clamped?

A repertoire of alternatives.
The eyes of a dog, large, following
each movement with credulous
Indifference, and cocking our
Ear for an inner voice
to tell us and the dentist
Where we are, how
To move.

Jovial, seasonal, and trite
the questions come, brief silence
ruined by his whistling meanwhile
and machines. What
Would you want for Christmas?
Where do you go to school?
What do you want to be

When you grow up.
The nurse accessory and smiling
Hands him cotton-balls.
Oh the misunderstanding is
Terrifying. They are whiter
than milk, than snow, than anything
already spoken for, over and over again.

His eyes are incapable
Of blinking and his teeth

stare white, hard
and straight.

It's over.
The clamps remove.
The loneliness impeccable,
Lively, a scattered rhythm
Everywhere pounding

SECOND SILENCE

I will enter my second silence.
I will watch
as small a flower as there is.

All the outsiders are solid.
My brothers collide with love
and anger; I grow weak
for my woods.

All round me: leaves.
I can care without sparing a word.
This is no way to witness a wedding.

I have no connections.
The sun is never lovely in my eyes.

Father: don't lend me your bridges.
They rot with sweet skill.

I will find my way among you.
My head is a roof to reflect
all your glances.
I am adolescent in my tongue – I love
and murmur mirrors

that slip swords from your wholeness.
Where will I come through?
How can I come in?

I am not bold.
I continue: lily
in bath of kindness –
                                        Your slyness.
                                        Someone in me knows.

My unlearned child isn't wild.
How pathetic, you child, how
Foul – how can I kiss you?
Your skin slides from my fingers.

I don't want you any more.
Please stand.
I have to go now.

I have a responsibility in silence.
It isn't snow, it isn't slow,
It isn't hell or heaven,
black or white.

This trip is wonder's baby:
Where's bravery?

It's sleek as a chestnut on the ground.
Quick as a fish standing still.

It has horses. It wears jewelry.
It knows.

The going is rocky lovely.
How shall I catch you, feather,
when you fall from those cliffs?

I will be broken then.
I'll be one-handed, firm
as pine – and grab you,
believing, and take you in,
your turn turning over

like a leaf in wind.

Clouds – I'm counting on a courtship
with your winds. I admire them.
I am jealous.

Time is my brother
who I've refused to see.
So long. Bitterness, you're a tyrant.
I'll meet him soon.
I'll know his face.
We'll embrace.

Prior: are these preparations?
Parodies, decked in bangles, chee-
cheeing on a string. What cheek.
What shall I do with
you monkeys, mine?

More.
There must be more.
More I can do, I can undo.

I will enter my second silence.
I'll stay here, but I'll go.
There are no exits –
I want it this way.

The sake is honesty.
Nothing can waver
where Truth stumbles along.
Left me maybe
the beginnings
of trees. Fir-trees.

Quick as a bird on a wire.
Quick as a mosquito on my hand.

My heart is stiff at games.
I haven't got what I was born with.
Pride turns shame because it isn't.
And shame burns to a stone.

The woods remain beautiful,
barren or pregnant.
Nothing changes.

What I love waits for me,
Unquietly.

I hope with a bullet in my teeth.
I hope with red berries like nuts
in my knees, my thighs.

I will seek my second silence
while I stay here crossing with you all.
I will see as small a flower as I am
turn into stone, to trees, to bones.

FOR WORDS

The whole English language
has decided to set up house
in my mouth and I tell you

There isn't room.
My mind will choke
My friends will be confounded
As I start stammering nonsense
Nude poetry, old bones, food
Unsuppressable giggles.

I'll sing London Bridge
While laughter bewilders
trying to convince everyone
I was right after all
There isn't room
My heart has decided to move out.

WITH THE POWER OF LEAVES

With the power of leaves
Self-conscious a dirty phrase now
What can't be stopped

The moon is not in the window.
The moon is in the sky
It is a pleasure to scuff through fallen leaves

To wake early and walk out.
My life with trees and so on
A friend arriving by surprise

Or singing while it snows on you,
the cool smart darkness, and know
In a way you're helpless, in a way not

A rush of hugs.
The water moves among the crowded rocks
Impatient well-being, before it's lost

Walks around, knocks on walls,
Breaks a few dolls, maybe.
People being electric, too

Turn on and off. And
the constant seduction of things taking you
In, wind, windows, doors, cracks

in sidewalks, clouds . . .
Situations
                photograph you
in their peculiar sweet sad

Nonsense
Prices of
Certain magical lines, crossed

Hello, goodby, names carried away
For we have laughed together, also
Getting truths off your back

But waiting
There is waiting in the air
A sense of waiting

Bend over sometimes the stream
and I cut my hands
into the water

                                        during a constant journey
Friend arriving by surprise
We are bewildered also
In a quiet way

Now and the power of leaves
Damp smell of woodsmoke
Soft, close, and drift

LIGHT IN YOUR KITCHEN

The light in your kitchen is enormous.
I'm tired of getting up in the middle of the night to bark at stars.
Now leaves whisper inside their trees.

What is this, a teeter-totter?
Come out of those skeletons rising.
The water carries a dead kitten; at night
the moon winks thru fast moving clouds.

It is not the words, like fault
But the vision they create
In the direction of the setting sun

Might as well point your nose
At your belly and howl.

I told myself to turn around
O the sweetness I wanted to eat
Because I was allergic. But

What is this teeter-totter? But
Look at the smile on their faces.
At the instant of recognition you turn
Into what was always there.
I will not leave because

The light in your kitchen is enormous.

MAY 1, 1970

Cold, pompous and manufactured Nixon
Told us about Cambodia. How
It was most right and decided to
Kill more, burn more, and maybe
There are no people in that place,
Just bases. Play ball.
And most of all don't forget
This is not an invasion, this is just
An invasion so far, not yet.
And how to see them, usurpers
in that place, and us
not to reveal the detached face
of the smart   passive   fat
Giant not easily piqued, the dummy
who won't defend its honor fast enough,
the gullible   gullible monster
fumbling the ball

Falls for Nixon's pass at the honorable hearts of us all.

PHOTO AT KENT STATE: MAY 4, 1970

You see her only in the process
of becoming a woman.
Her jaw will set early
and she'll learn early
in the climbing   lost
between legs, stretching for home

About the grief buried there
The knitted perpetual dark widow's hood
The monastic tenderness   spitting
In the world's face
Like a repeating rifle
The sweet beginnings of things.

Her face, a gulf
Desperately opening, causes
the explosion again and again
of an elegant sterile hotel
(as in the movie) in fire
and floating debris, America
His face, already sending out roots
Penetrating the dead sidewalk
Frightened, dreaming
Worms into the earth
Our earth
The one we sleep on top of

LIVING TOGETHER

It is raining
Again as we walk,
And in the advertising colorbook heart
of the newspaper a lightbulb
Hangs down

Into a sunlit meadow where
a woman stands in a newly designed dress,
Turns it on.

.
.

You bash
and insinuate your way in.
Bottles leak, delicate mirrors
Crash to the floor, even paper
Pictures fade in the dark
a bird sails through the livingroom

.
.

Move
this confusion, made as you go,
Mark trees, leave signs,
made as you go,
Make new places, leave
Even sweet secret histories behind,
Move to new places
Where we meet for supper
and our myriad embraces.

.
.

The water a net for daylight
and seen through leaves, from high up,
This windowseat a kind of slow snowfall
at dusk in powderspecks.

I designate three old lightbulbs
on the table, ours, a vague
Brilliance
to be considered in the form of pears.

.

.

We walk, as morning grows,
from car to field.
By a shack, sunflowers stand in rows.

Later, in corn, we inspect equations,
Dipping our toes in the mud rows.

There is a kind of glamour here,
Afterstorm drops on sheaves,
Stalks, and you are sitting

In my chair, smoking,
the idea of a goblet
of wine around your head.

.

.

On knowing the end of a line,
the edge of annoyance
or as the blackbird flies by
the windowseat.

Set the table first
in the crotch of an enigma,
between despair and the breakfast
Date after the primary gift
of flowers has melted into
a jar of slow swampwater
Stinking better than old night ngale eggs

.
.

(A spacious outhouse suspends exactly at the center of the picture It is attractively decorated elaborate detail inside and out This is to be surmised from the surface the frame is American gothic with ornate uprightness a small animal with wings and horns hangs over the edge of the door making the picture appear to be an allegory of the Protestant Revolution which it is not Vague shadows infest the first perspective In the lower left corner they are held together by an inconspicuous but essential wren which the artist apparantly intended for a miniature front lawn swan spouting water from its beak and carrying in one claw an hourglass which he did not After the bathroom in the far distance is a scene within a scene beware of convolutions a meadow exactly similar to the glass of water and a diffuse impression of flowers A faint intimation of perfection wafts sideways from the entrance of the museum across the canvas the third perspective is of almost presidential love)

.
.

And so
I'd emphasize any winning gesture
Against the already pointless curtsies
in the direction backwash.

Dangerous to behold,
Wonderful to imagine,
Beautiful to contain,

and better to send
with enduring postcards
to all your friends as the snow
fall shifts
and curls around lampposts
a minister in black slips
down the quiet street
with faint squeeks
Packs bootmarks in white sift.

.

.

A regular underground air force,
Pushing clusters of forget me nots
Out onto the overgrown lawn again,

A firm but gentle insistence.

.

.

The wonderful streaks on the ceiling tonight
that come from the crack in the door.

Seeds wait
in a grapefruit
I hear the laughter of
my friends and you at the door.

"Come on
to dinner, let's go"

.

.

In this postcard Jonah
is caught in the action of squatting

in a fish's mouth forever.
Formalized with flowers.
Persia, Herat, about 1425.
Between ornament and action,
An angel with one foot on the fish's back
Bears Jonah a green bundle,
resembling a funnel or another fish,
Clothes for the lord's servant.

There are letters mysterious to me
Written in Jonah's arms.

The sea is blue pattern of ringlets
Half-discovered circles
Rising on each other.

A tree
leans gently over Jonah's head
hang pears.
Or a yellow fruit resembling
genitals.

Jonah's naked fanny sits
out over the edge of the fish's jaw
and he is between a miraculous suspension
in water and firm foothold
in this triangular
and open mouth.

.

.

In a flash
the blackbird flies by the windowseat
in my head as we leave together
to eat. The walls of a room
had become ominous – we break
that with a stubborn insistence

Argue, tilting
again seated crosslegged in bed
naked, after a good, sweet one.

.
.

The intricate formalities of Persian art
make compassion awkward, but
that messenger with clothes
on the strict flatness of paper
seems to swing
across, as the fish arches in connection,
his five belly fins, feet, or wings.

.
.

How to end, to begin
as the snowfall shifts
and curls around lampposts,
and the pale maple, branches thrown out
in all directions, a long time,
their small red buds
appear
as cases opening like fists.

.
.

I gave too much to visual sense
and move now in new places
A third touch moves beside our own
Something fine bends over.

In this triangular and open mouth
between ornament and action
half-discovered circles

rising on each other
There are no teeth.

The walls of a room fade

In the dark a bird glides through

Cases open like fists

Half-discovered circles rise on each other
A firm but gentle insistence
Fixed in love where there are letters
Mysterious to me, inscribed in too many
pictures, and what is simple
quickly blends into the rest.

I don't think much anymore.
I live here.
I lie awake tonight.
I like it.

VISE

If I tread water –
Put me to sleep.

The long sleep they will know
I am styrofoam and
Will float.

If I tread water.

.
.

The war presides.
America upside down and inside out.

Thinking
is not a gracious enterprise.
Imagination –
I am afraid of you.

A rifle
Stares at me this very minute.
It has been with me for days.
It gives off ideas in rays of white light.
It says
        revolution
        repression
        sleep
        food
        history
        idiocy

It says
        idiocy
        history

sleep
food
repression
revolution

.

.

It is really in reverse
I carry my mother and father inside me
This,
and the smell of slow water
and a man carrying cartons of raspberries
tells me to get out of the way.

He goes
through the automatic grocery store door
into sunlight. His leaving
is like a dream, a piece
Remembered, wreckage.

.

.

To say anything at all
is to take part, and take apart.

I hold the afterimage
of one peach
in the green
grass, in the sun
Dear – I need it
Like a future.
It has been with me for days.

.

.

It is not dawn, passing
but the waiting I will be afraid of always.
Everyone almost knows this.

.

.

If I tread water
Put me to sleep.

They will know what I mean
I am styrofoam
and will float.

THE LADY'S DREAM, or SONG TO THE AMERICAN INDIVIDUALIST

Oh you are as sensitive as a computer
as strong as a white bull
as playful as a candle in a storm
as gentle as a wolf
with its young.

Not to know,
not to hear,
not to drift home with the tide.

You are as fearless as a cornered cowboy,
as solemn as an elephant, guarding
a wounded inferior (you think),
as innocent as any man of action could be.

Not to see,
not to touch,
not to nurse a wet wing underneath.

Oh you are as high as a flag,
as handsome as a skyscraper,
as delicate (if you only knew)
as rainwater.

Not to notice,
not to exaggerate,
not to harness a cardinal, a coyote.

You are as sure as a stone
as genial as butter
as straightforward as a knot.

You are in there.
You are in there.
I am going West.
I am going to you.
I am going West.

FOR AUGUST 6th, 1945

As I lie in my bed
I am queen of the elephants.
The blanket in shadows strewn
and rumpled around my right side.
It's growing like a squash plant
luxuriant, irregular, swelling.
I will never be eaten by crocodiles.
I am queen of the elephants.

That doesn't mean I myself am
an elephant. They are my
Friends. I ride the neck
of the oldest
one
(for he understands the most
 he is my chief advisor)
and I fit there
like a little horseshoe
precarious –
but my inexorable poise
keeps me from falling.
I belong there.

In my own body I
am not powerful
but the elephants are powerful.
They are
so much
that they will bring me to my rest
before the final war
so I will not have to see
the last faces of the dying
their fingers
burned into
their eyes.

ROCK MY BROTHER

Rock, my brother.

Now they cry out for you
Now they will open their mouths
Now they speak and meow,
Bellow and moo

A great tower, a sky
Scraper, they built
A concrete box,
A simple building, the snow clouds bulge
over it.
Flakes fall in large pieces tonight
The neon letters at the utmost top
Never blink but in the dark say
M - O - N - Y, a cryptic S
With a slash through it sits
In the center of the O

"Before we turn into cookies
  I want to say to this gathering . . . ."
"Sir, I interrupt because I feel . . . .
  It's time now . . ."
"Before we turn into cookies
  I want to say"
"Sir, but there are clearer ways
  To do this, I'm sure"
"Before we turn"
"But sir, there must – or more efficient"
God. God.
You with your one clean suit.

"We Americans have earned greatness
  We will use that greatness to
  Equally great uses

Everything is not perfect but we will cut
Out bad spots
All."

Time, my brother.
Who called on the phone and talked to yourself.
Who sat on the shelf with maddening implacability.
Who reflected the sun in the window,
Straightman, glass face, almost
Imperceptible rhythms,
Your speech, your speech.

Before we turn.
Taking a look, consider
"Sorry lady but there's a minimum speed
On this highway too."
Alice, you poor darling.
Take a look, consider
Sailboat directories, flower bulbs, earthenware
Pots, baby carriages, candlelight.
A minimum speed.
Give me something I can do right.

Turning turning turning and
Sphinxes at every corner yes

The silence on the moon is
Unimaginable – in his super spacesuit
Who can claim anything but strangeness?

Insufferable and silly crossroad
With the four way stop
And your moon silence
Without the necessary gravity
We turn into balloons,
Start fearing sharp edges
Again, especially those floating
With us around.

"See? See?" he said. "We're all in the same boat."
Simply what boat whatever comes
Happens to cross
Your mind
The ice tumbleth down
The bad spots sing in one body
The grass seeds with wind
The maggots thrive in the covered can
The time is right, die, fight

Rock, my brother.
The water curls around your waist.
Gently.. Scurry and hide,
The crayfish
Under you; the water curls.

It wouldn't be funny if it wasn't serious.
Have you seen that play?
Who could dare?
A hero, a hero.

"Aren't we all in our own little way?" she said
to the heads bending to hear
"No" he said, "we are not
  in the same boat at all
  But rather in different boats
  on the same sea."
But another said, "No.
  Different seas."
And he said,
"Correct, individual
  and common good."

Before we turn.
Take a look, consider
Gawain
Went up and put his head on the table
Bared his neck.

The Green Knight laughed.
"No, no" he said, "You
Chop <u>my</u> head off
First."

"Oh" said Gawain, shocked.
How long.
How long till my time.
The doctor tapped the knee
With a rubber hammer.
Minimum speed.
Who handles the deathwatch?
On the tower stands the hatchet.
An orange moon is suspended on the edge.
The sound of crickets rises
From the surrounding territory.
Crickets?

"One must have confidence competence
  Credibility conviction scarecrows" she said.
One must have oneself in one's fist.
The Green Knight laughs.

Rock, my brother.
You with your one rough face.
Scurry and hide, the crayfish
Under you. The water curls
Around your waist, gently,
Now. We.
Rock, my brother.
The music rides us we do not make it.

A swift transfer
Step right up and hurry
The twentieth century awaits
You
The ways are numerous
A lot is booming

There is a bird too
Gawain the maniac adhesive
Is easily disposed of
Don't be afraid of darkness
We have more lightbulbs than you can count
Don't be alone there are millions
Around you
Ah but wait
The voices in your head
Are not your own
They are a garden
They must be destroyed
First of all
Search and destroy
Don't wait for an apocalypse
We must be self sufficient
The signs are numerous
Wait patiently for the patient accumulation
Of signs
Are numerous
There was a sign
And it was surrounded by wasps
The noise was magnificent
And it was given a gun salute
And it said
Keep your cool.

The Green Knight laughs.
The night whispers
and the moon illumines
The long edge of a cloud.
The woman converses with a box of eggs,
The shopkeeper damns taxes,
The children play with water pistols
The cavern groans,
The lights go off
The red beacon flashes
The door slams

And the spider walks the rounds
Of his web.

An architecture
is obvious.
The cautious
Maneuver
oh so carefully
as they must
here and there
as they must
reach a space
to dance on
they do

The fly buzzes at the windowpane
This may be the only sound
As I sit here
in heat
in stillness

Who goes there
Walking the tracks at night
Dead alive and alive dead
Making mountains of cinder
Withholding from his god
His comfort and his bars
Are one
His foot
Nudges a rock embedded
in the track
and his hands
Stare at his face.

There was a dream
and the dream said
No.

The sun will not harm
The chicory, for they close.
Search for a shape,
Anything will do now,
and shall we go through all the shit
played backwards, or go on.
If played long enough anything
becomes cliche, yet
the familiar is too dear
for even those who cry for freshness here.

Time, my brother.
Stand by me in your confusion
and crossroads of the fourway
Stop and yield
with their moon silence architecture
with their cops and rebels
with their butterflies and bombs
with their communion and the bloody heads
Make me know
the newspapers are wrong
There is a chance.

The sun will not harm
The chicory, for they close.
I think I can touch you
for you are near.
The Green Knight laughs.
The red beacon flashes.
The fly buzzes at the windowpane
and the walls are concrete.

The doctor tapped the knee
with a rubber hammer.
Muscle muscle muscle
Bone bone bone.

Rock, my brother.
The music rides us we do not make it.

I would end my piece if I could.
It's long and I'm not sure it's any good.
Turning turning turning
and sphinxes at every crossroad yes
and dig it still the garden smells wet earth
turned over and worms worms moving in the mass.
There was a dream
and the dream said
No.
"Dip him in the river who loves water."
Gawain plays to the Green Knight's game.
He is eager to make a stand
but he isn't breaking any rules,
Rules that are never explained.
He imagines some mystery
to sustain himself.
The journey is long.
Where departure from yourself
Becomes arrival, and
Where arrival becomes departure
Infinite departures and
Not how close but
How liquid the distance
Between you and me.

The stuff of reality
can end now
Complete sudden
No one escapes.
No one will grieve   now
No one escapes   now
We have a star   now
In our hands   now
The sun will not harm
the chicory, for they close.

A new way of prayer
not fitting to an old way of action.
Who goes there, his hands
Staring at his face.
The walls are definitely made
of concrete
and the dream said
No.
Yes I believe it did.
Raindrops run down
the windowpane.
Water to sweeten
an abstract wound

WOOLWORTH'S

Oh I love the new Woolworth's.
The style so absolute and unashamed.
The moment I enter I am surrounded
pervaded
diffused
(This is the biggest in the country.)
I am a telescope.
I am a microscope.
I am a robot.
A new Beatles' song has been taken over
By men in business suits playing xylophones.
Ideas
Spring from ash-trays with a cat and
Six kittens all dressed in green. I think
I want a colored kerosene lantern
As tall as a pen. Plastic
Flowers bloom luxuriously in our midst.
Long legs
With tiny feet
Rise in the air delicately, from waists
Firmly cut off and planted in a counter.
They wear bright lime stockings.

ICE

It was around the waist of the day
We gathered hills in our pockets
Kept to ourselves, extraneous
Jokes meanwhile, soup-burns.
This must be a liquid time,
I thought, it has no change
Unless to freeze,
in which case we can crack
it into startling shapes by chance
And store it,
Inside us

The sensuous appeal
Of this as it forms in the stream,
On the pond, in patterns
Of white, off-white, gray
And the dramatic possibilities
Of it broken, angular

Feelings, maybe
Huge hunks of it floating
Bobbing, on the lake beyond
the cliff of whiteness, half-mile out,
Sways with waves, unsteady
Or, at some point
In the stream where dead tree
Or dam blocked the way,
A build up of jagged
Like entangled pyramids
Crushed together.

IN FORM

You move
in that half-light
of recent memory where I was
a bystander

There is no confidence in a line.
Protecting his territory a dog
Barks down the block,
someone pretends to live in silk,
another in cement, while we
Stick out our tongues at cameras.

Mowing down trees, they
have forgotten a road.

In the noble belch
all answers lie,
in the sigh of connection
we will gather like flowers to argue,
Wave, kiss each other out.

POEM

A circumstance of lips.
The sap knots,
Clusters on the bark.
Then do we slip into our streets like coins?

PORTRAIT

You've got something
I can tell
like a fern
Hanging out your back pocket.

Moved down the street
Wearily, dragging
Some invisible train of wooden ducks.

They sound in your ears
Not alone.
They have bells.
They waddle; they constitute an indignity.

There is a delicacy in your face.
Picking up traces of sky,
Your eyes.

SPRING EQUINOX, '69

Dear trees:

You rule the seasons.
And the changes.
And the subtle voices.
And the daily bread.
i know it.
Why these reversals?
This equinox portending winter follow spring.
And other things.
i have a list.
i insist.

For gumwrappers,
replace: ideographs.
i was beaten.
i hung
on a quiet x-ray.
He winked.
i smiled.

The big one is shadowy.
Please comfort me.
Although i have bones.
i made my home alone.
i repent.
Again and again.
The standing gestures stand.
But i fade behind them, i'm
after an insane paradise of freedom.
What i know is not viable.

Dismissed,
i bow down
Diffuse,

see more difference
Contráct,
rain   opens a chasm
and there's money there
to see us as unicorns
i haven't skill to catch
only sometimes compassion
Of course we forget our urges.
We'd burst.
We'd lose our jobs.

This
is the pattern of a gangster.
He sings.
He operates behind a front of busty witches.
There's a vast network
of underground treasure or
loot. Hand to hand,
accomplices in darkness,
wearing masks,
lone ranger style.
oh i have time.
i sleep in a cozy niche between minutes.
You can't connect something to anything.
You know that.
Make a decision, an incision.

Tree,
full of power,
flower of endurance
and intense indifference –
Why don't you speak to me anymore?
Have i broken the faith?
Are you dead?
Do i smell the onset of spring?
Have you no imagination?
Should i look higher?
What's my name?

Hey.

Sit with me
hold my hand
sit with me

This is downright slaughter.
i'm giving up dreaming.
The kitten's at the door,
wants in, wants food.

What's the light of head and womb?
The spectator's face was divided, a crease
Down the middle.
They switched the gigantic movie
to a small folding screen.
i tried to get a good seat.
He was scared,
So was i.
Divide and multiply.

All the perspectives were incomplete.
Bloodshed and bodies beyond recognition.
There's the dotted line across his forehead.
Where they operated.
Like a lid on a bowl, they took it off.
And put it on.
What happened then?
is happening now.
He couldn't move somehow.
A girl in the next row protested,
standing up and addressing the audience,
disowned the movie
as if it had to do with her.
The gates are frozen in.
The dictator is slim.

He says he means well.
i keep changing seats.
i'm giving up dreaming.
He is precise.
He is on time.
He buries his audience
in wars we cannot see
that hurt flesh
like all the others, again
and again.

Intact,
it goes on
Intimate,
shudders
            to the touch
Isolate,
steels
        itself for love
        for very love

HARD CATCH BY ECHO FALL

Hard catch by echo fall.

Did Sally bring in the rain pail?

Notice contortions.

A loaf of bread on the doorstep.

Have fun.

The saint holds his hand just so,
Delicate and special.

Toughness, would gentleness do better?

Would you like some coffee?

Nonsense, a child could do that, just so.

In fabric of time, a fish falls.

Don't forget to water the plants.

I'm sure, I'm very sure.

So many.

When are you coming home.

AD

Are you feeling blue?
Are you feeling gray?
Are you being pursued?

Take Anaro, break Anaro.

Are you feeling heavy?
Do you feel hot around the eyes?
Are you being scattered?

Take Anaro.
Everybody goes by Anaro.

Are you feeling inside out?
Are you feeling outside in?
Are you being watched, steadily,
by a mirror?

Make Anaro, take Anaro.

Are you feeling uptight, downright?
How many things do you want to fight?
Don't your windows let in any light?

Take Anaro, break Anaro.
I never use any other anymore.

WATER DREAM

In my dream
i stood
on a hill
looking over a lake
death in the air
it takes away
we don't know who
hold a party in defiance
have a baby
you are my brother
you are my sister
i've known you for years
where are you
i rush out
the boat
the boat
the boat will take
you away
down
i run down the hill
green grass
soft under my feet
the slope is long
                                        innocent summer
a small circle of water
                                        innocent stillness
the boat
the boat
swim to it
i rush in
Who do you think you are karen?
How could you possibly stop it?
There isn't even a sound.

My Aunt and i look over the water and green land
we stand on a gentle hill
the day is warm. sunlit. illumined.
she is a young woman alone, separate,
and proud, waiting
her delicate neck poised, bare
                                        innocent summer
                                        innocent stillness
the wind ruffles our wide full skirts
we are romantic
the grass is so green
it could break your heart
the aspen leaves twist
somersaulting at our backs
with every breath
                                    of air

i am swimming alone
in a dark place
snuggled into
the base of a mountain
the mountain
a great shadow here
or it is night
boulders are everywhere
scattered
about the pool
gray, wide, round
in clusters and alone
they've been arranged for me
this is my pool
the water is fresh, pure, black
the boulders tower over me
as i swim among them . . .

i think i'll be glad it's over.
i was so uncertain.
and i got tired a lot.

THE GARDEN

He is a tapestry woven into a pipe.
Below it hides
                    and corrects patterns in the dirt.
Those limpid sounds are not made
knowingly, and the right side finds
catastrophe
            splits in two the child.

His hand wakens me, a shape rich with substance again.
His flesh is a fountain I jump into.
He brings down my thoughts like birds.
A nest of minnows   wiggling
A fishbone of wheat   loosing kernels
the October damp sweetsmelling woods
and running water
among them, all of them
the great pipe's low groan
                                        speaking
fluid dark creamy secrets
ensconced like a fossil in a rock.

I'll be telling myself again
"Be quiet. Be still."
Oh how I will love him
when I have accomplished my will, my will.

No more the new thing and the new thing.
Questions are raised at the very beginning
By the first shoot, thus
am I interrupted. Where
will I go?
And in the first green shapes
so much is implied, remembering all
the old styles.

A shade shading
me, circles of lace
and heat
a garden of warmth
oh I will surrender in a meadow,
one I have smelled
                                        out of dry herbs.

Hold me and harrow me with wishes,
the language full
with small roses
because they were bountiful in that country,
and were not grown
                                        for vicious contest.